NATIONAL GEOGRAPHIC

Meet Jane Goodall

Robyn O'Sullivan

Contents

Meet Jane Goodall

Jane Goodall is known as the "chimpanzee lady." She has been watching and learning about chimpanzees for more than 40 years. Jane talks to people all around the world about chimpanzees. She wants people to understand and protect these amazing animals.

Jane Goodall has spent her life studying chimpanzees.

Dreams of Africa

Jane Goodall was born in England in 1934. As a child, Jane loved animals. She was very curious about animals and wanted to learn about them. When Jane was only 18 months old, she took a bunch of earthworms to bed. She wanted to see how they moved.

Jane spent lots of time outdoors. She watched the creatures that lived in her garden. She also spent time reading books about the jungle in Africa. Jane dreamed of living there some day.

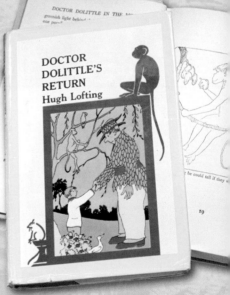

Books about animals and the African jungle were Jane's favorites.

When she was young, Jane dreamed about living in the African jungle.

NORTH AMERICA

England

EUROPE

ASIA

AFRICA

SOUTH AMERICA

AUSTRALIA

ANTARCTICA

After Jane finished high school, a friend invited her to go to Africa. Jane worked hard to save the money to go. When she was 23, her dream finally came true. At first Jane worked in an office, but she didn't enjoy this very much. She wanted to study animals. Jane's chance came when she began to work with Dr. Louis Leakey. This work changed her life.

Adventure in Africa

Dr. Leakey and his wife, Mary, were scientists. They studied **fossils**, which are the remains of living things that died long ago. Jane went with the Leakeys to hunt for fossils.

Dr. Leakey thought Jane would be good at **research**. Dr. Leakey told Jane about the wild chimpanzees living in a jungle **reserve**. He asked Jane if she would study them. She agreed to go. Jane's adventure in Africa had begun.

Mary and Louis Leakey hunt for fossils in Africa.

Jane lived in the jungle near the chimpanzees. She watched them every day. Jane saw the chimpanzees play together and **groom**, or clean, each other. She learned that they live together in families.

Chimpanzees groom each other every day.

Jane got to know the chimpanzees she watched.
They visited her to see where she lived.

Jane watched everything the chimpanzees did. Jane took detailed notes about everything she saw. Jane also took photographs of the chimpanzees. She realized it was important to keep notes. Keeping **records** is part of a scientist's work.

Jane used a notebook to keep records of everything she saw.

This chimpanzee uses a rock to crack a nut so he can eat it.

Jane discovered things about chimpanzees that no one had known before. She learned that chimpanzees use sticks and rocks as tools. They also use leaves as cups to get a drink of water.

Telling the World

Jane knew that not all chimpanzees lived as safely as the ones she studied. Some chimpanzees were hunted for food. Sometimes the babies were stolen and sold to circuses or pet stores. Other chimpanzees died because the forests where they lived were chopped down.

Jane offers food to an orphan chimpanzee.

These boys are planting flowers for their Roots & Shoots group.

Jane began to travel around the world teaching people about chimpanzees. She started many groups that work to protect chimpanzees and other wild animals. One program Jane started for children is called Roots & Shoots. This program teaches children how they can work to protect animals and their **habitats**, or homes.

Making a Difference

Jane's work helped to change the way people treat chimpanzees in the wild. Chimpanzees are now protected in many **national parks**. Jane's work changed the way zoos treat chimpanzees, too.

Zoos now keep groups of chimpanzees in large areas that are like jungles. The zoos also make sure chimpanzees don't get bored. Zookeepers give them things to do like hunting for food treats.

Jane Goodall is still telling the world about chimpanzees. They are her life's work. Jane's work shows us that one person can make a difference.

Jane still visits the chimpanzees in Africa.

Glossary

fossil   the hardened remains of a living thing that died millions of years ago

groom   to make clean

habitat   the place where a plant or animal usually lives

national park   an area of land set aside by the government where plants and animals are protected

records   written notes

research   to observe and study to learn new facts and information

reserve   an area of land set aside to protect plants and animals